Kirstenbosch

BEYOND WORDS

BRIZA

Kirstenbosch – BEYOND WORDS

PHOTOGRAPHS BY HARRIS STEINMAN

FOREWORD BY BRIAN HUNTLEY

INTRODUCTION BY CONNIE DE LA VEGA

Published by
Briza Publications
CK90/11690/23

PO Box 56569
Arcadia 0007
Pretoria
South Africa

BRIZA

www.briza.co.za

First edition, first impression 2007

ISBN 978-1-875093-85-4

Project manager: Douglas van der Horst
Copy editor: Douglas van der Horst
Design and layout: PETALDESIGN, Cape Town
Printed and bound by Tien Wah Press (Pte.) Ltd, Singapore

ACKNOWLEDGEMENTS

I am indebted to Connie de la Vega for her
persistence in pressing for this book to be published;
to Patsy Johnson for her loving support and guidance;
to my staff, Karen Horsburgh, Carine Davies and
Leoni Siebrits, for their valuable input; to Ernst van
Jaarsveld, Anthony Rebelo and John Manning for
their help with plant identification; and to the editor
and project manager, Douglas van der Horst, and the
designer, Petal Palmer, whose influence, direction and
skill have added impact and value to the work.

Harris Steinman

(Half-title page) *Euryops tysonii*
(Title spread) LEFT Fragrant spearleaf conebush
Leucadendron salignum **CENTRE** Protea leaves
RIGHT Langeberg pincushion *Leucospermum mundii*
(Imprint page) Common cabbage tree *Cussonia spicata*
(Contents page) LEFT Du Toit's conebush *Leucadendron
daphnoides* **RIGHT** Aloe leaves
(Page 6) LEFT Candelabra tree *Euphorbia ingens*
CENTRE Gold lobelia *Monopsis lutea*
RIGHT New leaves of honey flower *Melianthus major*
(Page 7) New leaves on proteas
(Pages 8 & 9) Featherhead *Phylica pubescens*
(Pages 10 & 11) Views of Kirstenbosch
(Page 12) Ribbon pincushion *Leucospermum glabrum*

CONTENTS

FOREWORD

KIRSTENBOSCH IS TRULY A GARDEN APART. All who have visited it, at any season, in any weather, cannot but be profoundly moved by its all-embracing beauty, tranquillity and presence.

South Africa is unusually endowed with floral treasures, spectacular landscapes and wild animals. We are indeed fortunate that much of this natural wealth has been secured for future generations within our numerous national parks and national botanical gardens. Despite the demands of often more pressing socio-economic priorities, successive governments have provided increasing support to our network of protected areas. The South African National Biodiversity Institute, which has its origins in the first national botanical garden established at Kirstenbosch in 1913, has a broad mandate from Parliament to promote the appreciation, conservation and sustainable use of our biodiversity.

Communicating the richness of the diversity of living things, of South Africa's extraordinarily wonderful Cape Floristic Region, its fynbos and forest, is a task that many a photographer has embarked upon, but few have met with such success as this photographic essay by Harris Steinman.

Five hundred years ago, Albrecht Dürer recorded the intimate details of a field of wild flowers, as might have been witnessed by a passing ant. Harris Steinman has brought us this closeness, his images revealing the diverse structure, pattern, colour, shape and delicacy of nature. Far too often we wander through Kirstenbosch at a pace that leaves no chance to examine the individual leaves, flowers, stamens, thorns or subtle colours of the garden's five thousand species of indigenous flora.

This elegant selection of fine photographic portraits allows us the opportunity to reflect on what we might have rushed past, perhaps, in order to reach our destination, without savouring every step of the journey through Kirstenbosch. For those who might need an incentive to move more slowly through the garden, to 'see more, talk less' as invoked by Bernard Takawira's great stone sculpture at the upper entrance to the garden, this volume is the perfect catalyst.

Brian J. Huntley
Chief Executive:
South African National Biodiversity Institute
December 2006

PREFACE

IN ONE OF HIS LECTURES JOHN CONSTABLE, the great English landscape painter, quoted the following lines from a poem by George Crabbe:

It is the soul that sees: the outward eyes
Present the object; but the mind descries.

When we walk around Kirstenbosch the physical act of seeing is modified and affected by all our other senses, as well as by subconscious memories and emotions of previous events in our lives. For one person a particular vista may stimulate recollection of an intense romantic interlude, while for another individual the same scene may generate feelings of displeasure. I have no doubt that every visual impression triggers an emotional response, possibly only unconscious and minor, but present nevertheless.

Such emotional responses are not only influenced by the whole scene but may be subtly adjusted by elements such as colour, shape, pattern or texture in our surroundings. The mood or emotion evoked may be brief and fleeting, but if one is able stay a while these feelings may grow perceptibly.

Edward Lucie-Smith, in *The Invented Eye*, pointed out that photography made it possible to '…bring time itself to a halt, to freeze the stream of moments, to choose an instant and keep it on record for ever…' In essence, the images in this book allow one to stay a while, to dwell a little longer; and I hope that they

will resonate with you in ways that are similar to the feelings I experienced when I captured them.

I have no idea how the images came about – I did not follow a predetermined plan or formula but over a period of several years responded subjectively to the visual impressions offered to me in Kirstenbosch: to the interplay between light and shade, to plant shape and structure, to colour, pattern and texture, and to the elegance, delicacy and tranquillity of the subjects. To put it simply, the images were created by my response to the wide range of visual impressions that were presented to my 'soul' or subconscious. When I framed them in my viewfinder, they simply felt 'right'.

The psychologist Carl Jung reminds us that a 'collective unconscious' binds us and is shared by all humanity. Subconscious common elements in all of us influence our responses to visual stimuli, even if we have had no previous personal experience of them. It is therefore possible that an image that caused me to stay a while may do the same to you, even if it stimulates a different emotion for no apparent reason. There is beauty even in imperfection.

If you are deeply moved by only one image in this book, then the flora and fauna of Kirstenbosch have successfully mentored me and allowed me to share their time with you.

Harris Steinman

INTRODUCTION

KIRSTENBOSCH NATIONAL BOTANICAL GARDEN is situated on the eastern slopes of Table Mountain in Cape Town, South Africa. It is part of the Cape Floristic Region, one of six 'floral kingdoms' in the world. It is the smallest of the six, covering just 90 000 square kilometres, but the region sustains over 8 600 plant species, making it the richest kingdom for its size and, some might say, the most beautiful of all. Seventy percent of those species are endemic, which means that they are found nowhere else in the world. About 1 500 of the species are found on Table Mountain alone, surpassing the total number of species found in the entire British Isles. The Cape Floristic Region was proclaimed South Africa's sixth World Heritage site by UNESCO on 30 June 2004. It comprises eight protected areas in the Western Cape, one of which includes Kirstenbosch. This is the first time that a botanical garden has been recognized as a natural World Heritage site – a recognition of the diversity and beauty of its plant life.

The garden was founded on land bequeathed to the nation by Cecil John Rhodes in 1902. In 1913 the Government set aside the overgrown farm of Kirstenbosch as a botanical garden with an annual grant of £1 000. Professor Harold Pearson, who had come to South Africa in 1903 as Chair of Botany at the South African College, became its first director, though he worked without a salary. He died in 1916 at the age of 46 and lies buried in the garden in the shade of a cedar tree. Another landmark, Colonel Bird's Bath, is named after a former owner of the farm, Colonel Christopher Bird, a deputy colonial secretary, who built the bath one hundred years before the establishment of the garden.

There are a number of plants in the garden that are extremely well suited to this part of South Africa, which has a Mediterranean climate but is often buffeted by storms, hence the nickname 'Cape of Storms'. The garden includes 36 hectares of cultivated plants, which are focused primarily on South African flora from the winter rainfall region of the country. Kirstenbosch grows only indigenous plants in its 528 hectares, which support a diverse 'fynbos' flora and natural forest. Because of its concentration on the species unique to this region, the garden plays an important role in protecting the native plant life of the Cape Floristic Region.

Fynbos species are typically found on soils that are poor or infertile, and depend on fire for regeneration. Adaptation to fire is either by re-seeding or re-sprouting. Those species that maintain

their populations by re-seeding have hard protective seed capsules that burst open following fires and release an abundance of seeds, many of which are carried underground by ants. They remain under the protective soil cover until conditions are optimal for germination, thus surviving the harsh post-fire conditions. Re-sprouters have large rootstocks or bulbs, from which new branches and flowers develop after fire. There are four main plant types in fynbos: proteas (proteoids), ericas (ericoids), reeds (restoids) and bulbous plants (geophytes).

Plants from the protea family were first recorded by a Dutch botanist in 1605 and were named after Proteus, the mythical son of the god Neptune, who could take on many disguises. They make up the larger shrubs of the fynbos. Africa is home to around 400 species of protea, about 330 of which are found in the south-western Cape. Only Australia with over 800 species has more.

The name erica is derived from the Greek word *ereike*, which means heath. The more than 600 species in the Cape Floristic Region are winter flowering and tender to frost. They appear as ground cover, in rock gardens, and as evergreen shrubs with small needle-like leaves and abundant, usually small, bell- or urn-shaped flowers. One South African shrub grown for its profusion of white flowers is interestingly named the Prince of Wales heath. With one or two exceptions, ericoids store their seeds in the soil.

Restios, a growth form unique to fynbos, are the ancient precursors of true grasses. They are evergreen reed-like plants, and though their flowers are small and unimpressive, their form, texture, and foliage colour create great interest in the horticultural world.

All 310 restio species are dioecious, which means that they have separate male and female plants, and the long-lasting seed heads of the latter are sought after. Ants are an important dispersal agent of restio seeds. In southern Africa, restios have been used as a thatching material for many centuries.

Geophytes consist of more than 1 400 species. Fynbos has the richest geophyte flora in the world, the Cape Floristic Region having 15–20 percent of the world's species. Appearing only in the wetter months, they survive the long dry summers, veld fires and animal grazing by dying back to their storage organs, such as rhizomes, tubers, bulbs or corms, and then sprouting anew the following growing season. Geophytes include various types of commonly known bulbous plants, such as gladiolus, lily and clivia.

Another interesting plant group is the cycads, which are survivors of ancient gymnosperms, and some genera are found only in Africa. Like the restios, each plant is either male or female, and they are pollinated by the wind or by insects. Some species are extremely rare and the collection at Kirstenbosch is used for research, education, and conservation. Plants are available to the public and are distributed to botanical gardens around the world.

Kirstenbosch is laid out in a number of sections that are crisscrossed by walks and adorned by large open lawns and wandering animal life – guineafowl and Egyptian geese are most visible, though raptors of various kinds fly above and smaller birds, such as sunbirds, can be seen throughout, often feeding in the flowers.

The Dell is the oldest part of the garden and features tree ferns and a wide variety of shade-loving plants, as well as Colonel Bird's Bath and Pearson's Grave. The Colonel's bird-shaped bath, which is constantly replenished by a natural spring, is in one of the most beautiful parts of the garden, surrounded by ferns, and permeated with a sense of tranquility. The Camphor Avenue, made up of trees planted by Cecil Rhodes in 1898, is an impressive feature in the lower part of the garden. Other sections bear the names of plant types: Fynbos Garden, Erica Garden, Protea Garden, and Restio Garden. One area concentrates on vygies, which are succulent plants that bloom profusely in October. The Koppie exhibits tough, drought-resistant plants that survive on its well-drained sandstone. Van Riebeeck's Hedge was planted in 1660 as a boundary when the Cape Colony was established, and now adorns part of the path leading to the Matthews' Rockery, where succulents from the arid regions of South Africa are displayed. The rockery was built in the 1920s, using many wagon loads of rocks and sandy soils to provide very well-drained conditions for the succulents to survive in Kirstenbosch's moist micro-climate.

The garden also includes a conservatory, an arboretum, and a sculpture garden with a collection of works from the Shona sculptors of Zimbabwe. There are also demonstration gardens that allow visitors to learn about the various plants and their uses, and how to create water-wise gardens that require less maintenance. A Cycad Amphitheatre features the plants that were of such great interest to Professor Pearson. In summer, concerts are held on a vast expanse of lawn that slopes down to a covered stage.

Large parts of the garden are uncultivated, and in these areas there are paths for walking and hiking. Kirstenbosch is a favourite starting point for hikes up Table Mountain, the summit of which is more than 1 000 metres above sea level. Deep gorges and four streams grace the mountain and the ascent to the top rewards the hiker with spectacular views of Cape Town, its suburbs, and the surrounding oceans.

Professor Pearson's epitaph has provided many visitors with valuable counsel for approaching the garden: 'If ye seek his monument, look around you.' Harris Steinman's images of Kirstenbosch pay tribute to this sentiment. While many who have published books about the garden were interested primarily in the biological aspects of the plants or the large-scale scenic beauty of the setting, Dr Steinman has searched for subjects that elicit a range of characteristics and moods, and has arranged his photographs according to the shape, colour, structure, pattern, texture, delicacy and elegance of the plants, as well as the feelings of tranquility evoked by the flora. His lens reveals aspects of the plants that we seldom notice and exposes us to nature's artistry that is, indeed, beyond words.

Connie de la Vega

COLOUR

PREVIOUS SPREAD King protea *Protea cynaroides*

ABOVE Seed capsules of falling stars *Crocosmia aurea*

Bush-willow tree *Combretum erythrophyllum*

ABOVE Parachute daisy *Ursinia cakilefolia*

RIGHT Lightning bush *Clutia pulchella*

OPPOSITE Mountain dahlia *Liparia splendens*

LEFT Heath *Erica* sp.

CENTRE Fonteinbos *Berzelia lanuginosa* (dead bush)

RIGHT *Thesium* sp.

LEFT Dwarf coral tree *Erythrina humeana*

RIGHT Bitter aloe *Aloe ferox*

OPPOSITE Coral tree *Erythrina caffra*

OPPOSITE Pig's ears *Cotyledon orbiculata* var. *oblonga*

LEFT Oily conebush *Leucadendron glaberrimum*

RIGHT Kei cycad *Encephalartos princeps*

PATTERN

PREVIOUS SPREAD Pincushion *Leucospermum cordifolium x tottum*

OPPOSITE Overberg pincushion *Leucospermum oleifolium*

LEFT and RIGHT Purple wild tibouchina *Dissotis princeps*

ABOVE Oily conebush *Leucadendron glaberrimum subsp. erubescens*

OPPOSITE Pincushion *Leucospermum* sp.

OPPOSITE Coulter bush *Athanasia crithmifolia* **ABOVE** Coffee bush *Brunia albiflora*

FOLLOWING SPREAD: LEFT Pompom tree *Dais cotinifolia* **RIGHT** Buchu *Agathosma* sp.

SHAPE

PREVIOUS SPREAD Corkscrew flower *Strophanthus speciosus*

ABOVE Western sunbush *Leucadendron sessile*

OPPOSITE Spicy sunbush *Leucadendron tinctum*

LEFT Limestone sugarbush *Protea obtusifolia* **RIGHT** Rocket pincushion *Leucospermum reflexum*

OPPOSITE Common sunshine conebush *Leucadendron salignum*

OPPOSITE Conebush *Leucadendron* sp.

LEFT Gousblom *Arctotis* sp.   **CENTRE** Spicy sunbush *Leucadendron tinctum*   **RIGHT** Yellow rocket pincushion *Leucospermum reflexum* var. *luteum*

LEFT and RIGHT King protea *Protea cynaroides*

OPPOSITE Jade plant *Crassula ovata*

TEXTURE

PREVIOUS SPREAD **Elim conebush** *Leucadendron elimense* subsp. *elimense*

LEFT **Red crassula** *Crassula coccinea* RIGHT **Lesser candelabra tree** *Euphorbia cooperi*

Sandveld spiderhead *Serruria decipiens*

ABOVE **Cape scabious** *Scabiosa africana*

OPPOSITE **Langeberg pincushion** *Leucospermum mundii*

OPPOSITE Ribbon pincushion *Leucospermum tottum*

LEFT Rocket pincushion *Leucospermum reflexum* CENTRE Picketberg conebush *Leucadendron discolor* RIGHT King protea *Protea cynaroides*

LEFT **Overberg pincushion** *Leucospermum oleifolium* RIGHT **Limestone sugarbush** *Protea obtusifolia*

OPPOSITE **Blue squill** *Merwilla plumbea*

STRUCTURE

PREVIOUS SPREAD **Crane flower (bird of paradise)** *Strelitzia reginae*

ABOVE **Ribbon pincushion** *Leucospermum glabrum*

OPPOSITE **Gousblom** *Arctotis hirsuta*

LEFT *Euphorbia ledienii*   RIGHT Seed capsules of large wild iris *Dietes grandiflora*

OPPOSITE Coffee bush *Brunia albiflora*

OPPOSITE Flame lily *Gloriosa superba*

LEFT Coral aloe *Aloe striata*   CENTRE Red hot poker *Kniphofia* sp.   RIGHT Fountain pincushion *Leucospermum grandiflorum*

TOP LEFT **Bredasdorp conebush** *Leucadendron laxum*   TOP RIGHT **Tree pagoda** *Mimetes fimbriifolius*

BOTTOM LEFT **Common pagoda** *Mimetes cucullatus*   BOTTOM RIGHT **Ribbon pincushion** *Leucospermum glabrum*

OPPOSITE **Medusa's head** *Euphorbia caput-medusae*

Delicacy

PREVIOUS SPREAD Mallow *Anisodontea julii*

OPPOSITE Heather *Erica* sp. LEFT Sea pink *Limonium capense* CENTRE Heather *Erica* sp. RIGHT Mountain heather *Erica corifolia*

Rose scented geranium *Pelargonium capitatum*

Silver-edge pincushion *Leucospermum patersonii*

OPPOSITE **Kogelberg pagoda** *Mimetes arboreus*

LEFT and RIGHT **Featherhead** *Phylica pubescens*

OPPOSITE TOP LEFT Pincushion *Leucospermum* sp.   TOP RIGHT White arum lily *Zantedeschia aethiopica*

BOTTOM LEFT Milkbush *Euphorbia mauritanica*   BOTTOM RIGHT Bredasdorp conebush *Leucadendron laxum* (new growth)

ABOVE LEFT Gousblom *Arctotis stoechadifolia*   ABOVE RIGHT Bredasdorp conebush *Leucadendron laxum*

Coulter bush *Athanasia crithmifolia*

Periwinkle *Vinca major*

Elegance

PREVIOUS SPREAD Wild garlic *Tulbaghia violacea*

ABOVE Cape daisy *Dimorphotheca ecklonis*

TOP LEFT River lily *Crinum macowanii* **TOP RIGHT** Carpet geranium *Geranium incanum*

BOTTOM LEFT *Streptocarpus rexii* **BOTTOM RIGHT** White arum lily *Zantedeschia aethiopica*

Broad-leaf featherbush *Aulax umbellata*

Convolvulus sp.

LEFT Bredasdorp conebush *Leucadendron laxum* **RIGHT** Flame creeper *Combretum microphyllum*

LEFT Fynbos aloe (bergaalwyn) *Aloe succotrina* **RIGHT** Overberg pincushion *Leucospermum oleifolium* hybrid

Tranquility

PREVIOUS SPREAD *Chironia linoides*

LEFT *Leucadendron* hybrid   RIGHT *Leucadendron tinctum* hybrid

LEFT Broad-leaf featherbush *Aulax umbellate*   **RIGHT** *Leucadendron* hybrid   **FOLLOWING PAGE** Buchu *Agathosma* sp.

PREVIOUS PAGE Downy jasmine (star jasmine) *Jasminum multiflorum*   **ABOVE** Ana tree *Acacia albida (Faidherbia albida)*

Scabious *Scabiosa columbaria*

OPPOSITE Cape chestnut *Calodendrum capense*, Parachute daisy *Ursinia cakilefolia* (foreground), Boer bean *Schotia* sp. (background)

ABOVE Gousblom *Arctotis hirsuta*

Stream at twilight